BONEYARN

BONEYARN

poems

David Mills

THE ASHLAND POETRY PRESS

Printed in the United States of America
ISBN: 978-0-912592-86-2
Library of Congress Card Catalogue Number: 2020935743

Cover art: Nicholas Fedorchak
Cover design: Nicholas Fedorchak
Editing: Deborah Fleming

Acknowledgements

Thanks to Mom and Dad for holding fast.

Dorothy White—friend and now ancestor—and the Queens Council on the Arts for the grant that gave rise to this project's early words.

Tim Seibles, mentor/friend, who I'd told, after fulfilling the grant, "the poems keep coming; I'm even jarred from sleep by them." "That's the ancestors needing you to tell more of their story," he said. "Be still and listen."

To a poetic troika, a brilliant, bighearted brain trust: Connie Voisine (never would have made it without you), Rodney Jones, and Alan Shapiro—thanks for early and subsequent eyes on these words and for keeping in touch.

Mrs. Betty Holden for a second literary wind.

Grandma Elaine, who, two months before she died, said, "Dee (my nickname) keep writing, I had a dream about a poet being in our family."

Ellen Bryant Voigt, Paige Webb, Dr. Fleming and Dr. Rathbun for believing.

Uncle Harold, Aunt Pen, my *little* brother "Big D," Cuz, Tracey Capers, Langston Hughes, and Sean Ghazala for giving me inestimable creative and critical latitude at the African Burial Ground.

Howard Pflanzer—deep ties/critical eyes my friend.

Jill Klein, Jeff Allen, Rose Auslander, Robert Bensen, Marita O'Neill, and Jennifer, for your *bonhomie* and multiple minds' eyes on these poems.

John Davis for righting my childhood ship.

Carol Fox, Pradeep A., Ruth, Mishie, Mona, V, Danny Dan, Boobi, Cyn, Alicia, my sands, especially Derrick, Mike and Clint.

Terrance Hayes, Van Jordan, Toi, Maya, Anselm Berrigan, Lynn Lobell, Brooks Haxton, George Hovis, Jessie W., Craig Friend, Mr. Hawkins, the African Burial Ground National Monument, Phyllis Wat, M. Scott, Lee, Rod, Ezra, Chisholm, Galway Kinnell, Joan Digby, Rusty Duncan, Phil Young, and Norman Stock.

The infinite spirit through which all is possible. And most importantly to the 15,000 enslaved ancestors buried in Lower Manhattan, thank you for letting me sing a few notes of your necessary and too-oft-forgotten song.

Many thanks to the editors of the following publications where these poems first appeared:

African-American Review: "Buttonwood Agreement"; "Nail and Pine" (published as "13 Caskets: 13 Would-be Colonies"; "Talking to the Bones (*Had you abandoned baby talk?*)"; "Talking to the Bones (*What harbors the pain?*)"

Boog City: "Sundered"; "Talking to the Bones (*But what of the North?*)"

Bridging the Waters: An Anthology of Korean and American Poetry: "Talking to the Bones: (*Why bury the pate facing west?*)"

Brooklyn Rail: "A Clockwise Tizzy"; "Construction"; "Full Out: *Richard*"; "An Honorable Harvest"; "This Is Sorcery"; "To the Bones: About the Beads: Talking (*The one-hundred-plus waist beads strung around your midriff?*)"; "Which, Too/Split Flash: Break"

Colorado Review: "Coating: *Warwick*"; "Feet-Me-Downs"; "First and Final"

The Common: "Breath's Breath"; "Long in That Late Afternoon Light: *Bukay*"; "Talking to the Bones: (*What of the way of your demise?*)"

Crab Orchard Review: "Assignment"; "Deem Me: Piter/Pater"; "Telling Time" as "Murder's Milk"

Diode Poetry Journal: "Bless This House: *Peggy*"; "Which / One: 1712 Slave Revolt"

The Inflectionist Review: "To the Bones: About the Beads: Talking (*That clear glass bead with a clear green heart in your grave?*)"

Jubilat: "Knuckles of Smoke" as "Down Below Say-So"; "Mercy"

Konch: "To the Bones: About the Beads: (*On your right wrist, why the bracelet of turquoise and yellow glass beads?*)"

Kweli Journal: "After/thought/After/life"

The Literary Review: "An Almost Audience" as "The Almost Audience"; "The Apprentice"; "Colonial Cemetery"; "Talking to the Bones (*What of your face?*)"

Live Magazine: "August and the Law: *Sandy*"; "Talking to the Teeth: (*Now you are one with a skull: its white hush*)"

Main Street Rag: "Talking to the Bones (*Of the nine Akan beads in the entire cemetery, eight yellow beads were around a two-month old's neck?*)"; "Talking to the Bones (*Who did this?*)"

Newtown Literary: "Kin: *Quack*"; "Kith" as "Fair Trade"; "Sable Marginalia"; "Scribble: Jupiter Hammon"

Obsidian: "The Body Is a Metropolis"; "Negro Chimney Sweep"; "A Six-Sided Cedar Coat"

Piltdown Review: "*Whistlelo*"

Posit: "Talking to the Bones (*Had you made Joshua Delaplaine's acquaintance Mr. Castins?*)"; "Talking to the Bones (*What of only chimneys and flues?*)"

Taint: "Ashley and New Amsterdam"; "Auction: Hell's Unbidden Hello"; "Day's end."; "Snagging Shadows"; "Tinged"

In remembrance of the 15,000 unnamed enslaved and free blacks, indentured whites, and Native Americans interred in New York City's Negro Burial Ground, America's oldest and largest slave cemetery: 1712–1795

Contents

BONEYARNS

JUPITER & WHEATLEY'S SUITE

FREEDOM SUITE

"Ghosts of all too solid flesh,
Dark ghosts come back to haunt you now, . . .

I am the American heartbreak"

—*Langston Hughes*

PRELUDE

Colonial Cemetery

And they conferred together and with the money bought
the Potter's Field as a burial place for strangers.
—Matthew 27:7

Earth off-limits to the bones-of-who

                owned by the bones of who

could attend Trinity Church

                Earth off-limits

to the bones of who

                they owned. *The bones*

of whom?

Assignment

There'd been the donated the unclaimed
the criminal. At times when the North fell
short the South packed bodies in hogshead
casks. With enrollment bloated on Robinson
Street, Kings College became Columbia.
That once one-room schoolhouse joined

at Trinity Church's hip had a new name
and address in the new republic—the hither
to now the hereafter. How did medical school
students ply their jarring art and crafts when
the student body had grown yet the dead
bodies had not? The city's graveyards:

off limits to paupers and Negroes
and seldom pawed by resurrection men.
There those that loved those who'd left
visited regularly, had mortsafes, guards.
Death separated men by class and sweat.

February 3rd, freedmen's petition: *Sirs,*
most humbly, young students of the physic,
under the cover of the dual darkness—the night
and the heart's—during merciless sallies
repair to our grounds. We know we are not
to congregate at night but take risks to cloak

loved ones. These students too often
interrupt our Earth. Our fallen no
mere specimens but deeply cared for
deeper than the graves they're buried
in. If students cannot cease we seek
decency. Yet white lads in wool

suits skulked cold, moonless streets past
hunched sacks of rubbish to the boneyard—
grave riflers seeking recently-turned earth;
the newly deceased in winter when death intended
to keep bone and organ banded. In haste they filched
knowing decay worked nearly as fast. To keep

stones from crying out, they uncorked coffins
with wooden shovels, returned the earth
hauled their borrowed quarry to class. This
was sure. This was cheap. This was studying.
This was hit these bodies as if they were
books. This was an open secret anointed

by the elite—autopsy's insights, like New York's
expansion, built on captive backs. No telling
how many Negro cadavers those too-young sons
of Galen harvested when the city's one scalpel school
was just muddy cobbles from the Burial Ground.
Here, the nearby—and in life, the neglected—

anatomical fodder. Columbia's labs and classes
or New York Hospital's not-for-credit courses
their final resting place. Here no post-mortems
to isolate conditions loved ones could shirk.
Just anatomical abattoirs festooned
with black cadavers; corpses mangled

by curiosity and sternal saws, bubbling in bake-
kettles, harpooned genitals; bone spurs sandwiched
between the headboard and linen of a student
cot. Sacrilege for Christians who believed only
an unbothered body could twinkle in the Kingdom
of God. But the deceased no longer needed

to accost the blood's troubling sugar: so what if
a gallbladder was gone; a pancreas pawned; who
cared if the legislature passed a "bone bill." The dead
had no standing as property. Only two-legged real
estate could've properly been considered property. Hell
at the end of the day, they were just homework.

Telling Time

Head left. Jaw hoverin' above

that same shoulder. Right shoulder

pressed against my coffin: one

baby's casket just 'bove my

heart. Another baby on my right—

coffin waist high reachin' for

an ankle that no longer is. Trinity.

Three coffins: one grave. Snug.

These infants mine as we told time:

time to go. And in they own sweet

time, death inspectors tell me

I'm 'tween 25 and 30. *Say*: one

of my children never knew two months.

Say: the other 'tween half a dozen

of those and a year. *See*: all of us

now mothered by mother earth

and murder's milk

I

Chimney Sweep Apprentice

I'm what happens when a house breathes
out: sore black breath in a New York throat.
Trapped caterpillar. What they think
of me—owners of these homes
and white master who hires me out

to black master sweep. Elbows ankles
knees up zig-zag chimneys: squeeze
of heat and dusk. Soot head to toe: dirt
thick as a shirt. Palms facin' out; stomach
up against and empty. My days a brick

wide and a brick and a half long: I could
die here. But brush above my head
I chuck soot; chip tar wit' a scraper;
black rain pepperin' my neck hot rim
of my eyes. Filth to the sides of flues

mazes sticky with poison, hearth
to cap damper. Started prenticin'
when I was six.   Now
eighteen. Flesh leathery. Ankles
swelled to black apples. Growin':

a stunt. Can't say which is better:
cramped heat or winter's chill.
My cry—*Soot-O Weep Weep*!—
on the street or pinched in the flue.
My life up in nothin' but smoke.

Talking to the Bones: Chimney Sweep Apprentice

What of only chimneys and flues?
This: the one moment master permitted
me to be above him

How so?
Only in filth could I gain favor

Did you ever dream?
Things like thoughts weighed
too heavy on my head

How should you be remembered?
The neck a storm; the head a cloud
unsettled by its own weather

Talking to the Bones: Columbia Graverobber Victim

Who did this?
Abuse's students

Why?
Med'cin drives some men
to unbutton their monsters

But why put the crown of your head in the crook of your arm?
They sawed bone to what
they thought was thoughts

They discovered and exhumed for what?
Life had already taken my life
med'cin just cracked open its questions

Mercy

Indeed, I tremble for my country when I reflect that God is just.
—Thomas Jefferson

Along the city's jawline by
the wharf where a peck of slaves
were auctioned, Claus might have

heard tell how Robin sunk a penny-
knife into the conch below his
owner's shoulder. Now barefoot

he is stripped to the waist spread-
eagle, bound to a wagon *wheele*:
spokes versed in grass and its green

obedience; mud's scorched metamorphosis;
the way snow delivers news piecemeal
from the heavens. Limbs stretched

slowly rotated on that wheel, Claus
absorbs the dust, the turns, the deliveries:
each journey's leg and arm. Executioners

seldom traffic in compassion;
this one punishes Claus bottom
up. First a sledgehammer rains

on his shins—*Jesus have mercy, he
screams and rotates*—until they snap
between gaps of the wheel;

a wooden cudgel sings
to his kneecaps—*he howls
rotates*—'til they shatter . . .

Even the chalky taunting throng
winces. Then the thunder of an iron
bar's administered to his forearms

—*he shrieks, rotates*—'til they're smashed. . . .

The elbows/the chest/the endless bone-
cracking caught a quarter mile off. Until,
against God's own architecture, each

limb dips like a fractured hammock.
On the Commons between Broadway
and Kip, the wheel's nailed high on a pole.

Sparrow-hawks peck at the broken body.
For four days—for likely only having
offered Robin a penny-knife or shelter

in the wee hours of an April morn—
he is bloody billowing laundry
only death has the stomach to dry

CELLARS AND ATTICS

Knuckles of Smoke: *Peggy*

I got dark authority. Some down below
    and a bit-of up-above say-so. Shop
and sometimes sign for Master. Mostly
    I spice stir stew and boil. I rule

as salty beads crouch on my top lip;
    I stoop and bury sweat in my striped apron.
My body bakes and roasts while baking
    and roasting mutton and sweetmeat

With all these smells—cured fish:
    its salty kick—a nose is mostly on
its own down here in this clammy
    dark. My world ruled by mean

heat and knuckles of smoke:
    hours of kindling fire, bake
kettles swaying from pothooks, grimy
    spits turning, flames flaming, coals

raked. Grunt. Drag a cast-iron pot
    onto a bickering pile of them. Guide
that wood shovel: handle long as Big
    John's arm. Ease some tarts in that

oven's gut. Everything boils
    down to heat. Some fire
place bricks: the color of bone.
    Simple. Black bread only rises

to a point, like me climbing
   the mistress' stairs setting
my simm'rin living just
   shy of her shut door

Bless This House: *Peggy*

Backstairs twistin' like my braids
  every time I gently place tray
    after hot tray on that dusty top
      step. My bulky reflection tangled

in the platter's words: "Bless This House."
  Must be only the Miss's part it's talking
    cause there's little *blessed* livin'
      in this here cellar. But she and me

got the hours straight—*eights, twelves, sixes;*
  Sundays' sixes is five—when the tips
    of my fingers tap my side of the door.
      Wait. Tap again 'til I hear her clear her throat

Then I know the mistress knows their eats
  is ready. In their world—where people
    only belch and dream—rest of her
      family think supper just shows up

Whistlelo

Freedom? I live in a lawyer's clamped
    attic with Minnie and Cudjoe
who ain't free. Same much the same

    they do behind the lawyer's bolted
doors. Also cain't vote, testify, no
    ponderin' on a jury. No rights.

    Slave codes. They fought
because of tax sum'thin without
    reprezintashin. Where's my war?

Negro Chimney Sweep

Down here: blankets we have to collect soot become the blankets we use
to collect sleep. But just before dawns, temperatures would dip. Brush and
scraper slung over our underfed shoulders; sweep caps clutching our necks.
We'd head 'long Pump Street past Catherine Lane. Scorchin' morning
with our yawps, we'd snap dawn's silence: *Sweep-O Sweep!* Master Tobias
headin' us to 'cute angles and dirty work—to owners who'd wait 'til the fat
cooking of Christmas 'til their weep holes almost choke on suckling pig
and *Yorksure* puddin'. But I'm hardly fed—

my stomach howlin' means his poke fatter. Life: nothing but to and fro.
Bushels of soot packed in twilight dragged from hearth to courtyard;
fertilizer for yeoman sifted for lumps; money from dust in master's
pocket. Sticky stuff in a blanket. Emptied and filled. Again and again. No
Franklin Stove in this cellar: so I huddle with other apprentices for heat.
What was my bag by day becomes my bed by night. My tattered breeches'
waistband turned down—a pout. Ease out of 'em. Underwear or buff it?
Buff it. Even in this cold—gummy puffback on my flung

drawers. My calves. My clothes, skin and cover covered with soot.
Blackened blanket on top blackened blanket underneath. Me between:
a burnt sandwich. Sore. Swellin.' Wheezin.' Sleeping in the black. Spine
wrenched. My should-be-blooming bones squashed from twist and
scrunch; limbs wrung from heavin' bags of soot twice my teeny self. Stuff
peppers my throat, snakes to my gingambob. Memories: is embers hot and
glowing in my head

August and the Law: *Sandy*

Sickness now a light sleeper
                              Chimney and oven
weavin' heat to more heat. Some

                 time just easier to curl up outside
Late summer so sticky: August

                 and sleep should be outlawed

Snagging Shadows

Being only part ways undergrounds, our eyes
grab shadows, like those of them wishbone chimneys

                    beyond Master's house. Our ears

catch the *cluck cluck* of dashing brogans. White world
above us at ease: livin' in and stompin' on our heads

THE BODY'S METROPOLIS

The Body Is a Metropolis

I.
Through a chilly side door opening
onto Jews' Alley, Caesar slipped
into Hogg's shop palmed silver linen

and pieces-of-eight, squirreled housewares
under his master's floorboards. But
robbery turned to conspiracy when

Irish Mary claimed—that February
at Hughson's tippling house, hunched
over leg-of-mutton and drams of rum—

Caesar, six other Ethiops and Hughson
hatched a plan to start at the Fly
Market and paint the city in flames:

for the slave codes, the stop frolic
the no stroll after church-out.

And just like the goose Hughson had Mary
serve those sable grains of Ham, she swore
those men would be cooked—on *both* sides.

Echoing an April nearly three decades earlier:
May. Shadowy glen betwixt Windmill
and Potbaker's Hill. That last thieving winter still

with Caesar—the *Nigra* emperor—when from
the gallows, for the burglary, he's cinched.
Floor refused his twitching feet. His body

a weapon turned against him. Its weight:
as if he were standing on his jaw. Never
confessed. Pride: father of pigheaded death.

II.
But Caesar's ending ended again.
                    Drooped
for light and heat they couldn't
pin on him. Cut down. Rehung.
Swinging in chains from a gibbet
on an isle in the Little Collect.

A body left to rot is a message and a metropolis:

Caesar's head was a blaze, a March 18th, his thoughts: Ft. George;
Caesar's pate was Wednesday the harbor viewed from a hill,
chapel bells, a lull of wood, gunpowder that could've blown but
the Fort burned down because of a plumber's soldering iron

Caesar's tongue was a soon quench, a Captain's house near the
Long Bridge, a March 25th the faulty chimney's fault

Caesar's shoulder was a warehouse by a dockside owned by Van
Zant; Caesar's shoulder had a haystack, was a deal board near the
East River; Caesar's shoulders were three fires *three* Wednesdays

in a row, was an April 1st to the ground burned and a little fishy,
was what would another Wednesday have in store: pinned on a
corncob pipe

Caesar's kidney was a cow stable at the Fly Market, dusk on April
4th; Caesar's kidney was alarming, a Lane of Maidens where roofs
were palms and smoke never got out of hand or haystack; Caesar's
kidney was getting suspicious. Was proof. Of the fact. That fear.
Shares three letters. With fire.

Caesar's spleen was nearby and soon thereafter, a cry of fire before
old smokes cleared; Caesar's spleen was a flicker, a loft where slaves
slept; Caesar's spleen was soon extinguished and Thomas' place.
Was arson—as African art

III.
John Hughson: bobbing, Irish potato
in an Anglican pot. Hughson—scrawny
in a city bloated with property owners—
fenced stolen goods for the Geneva Club
Negroes; hid coins for Caesar that Caesar
had pocketed. But when the court offered

loose-lipped Mary freedom, she couldn't credit
the enslaved with spearheading the plot. Hughson—
her boss—had to emboss the ring. Her words
wrung John's neck. Final ride from the city, warty
tree toads chortling: Hughson standing tall

IV.

Chained to a gibbet beside Caesar

Hughson also gave up his own ghost twice:

another carcass left to rot: memorandum to a metropolis

Hughson's mouth was Sunday morning, Murray's coach house,
was nestled coals in a haystack; Hughson's mouth was April 5th on
lower Broadway, was a trail of embers snaking to the neighbor's;
Hughson's mouth was a mild suspicion of a Negro in there;
Hughson's lips were proud parents letting their fire go out. For the
first time. On its own.

Hughson's lung was four more fires all on Monday. *that's not true.*
Hughson's lung was 10 a.m. was Burns' chimney.

Hughson's neck was two hours later, was Hilton's roof just east of
Sarly's, was up in flames. Was Evidence.

Hughson's tear ducts were vigilantes, Monday's interruption;
Hughson's tear ducts were magistrates, Spanish Negroes and four
o'clock; Hughson's tear ducts were take a seat but give it back:

because Hughson's liver was an alarm in a warehouse on New
Street; because Hughson's liver was fire on a shingle's heels where
smoke tottered; because Hughson's liver was a Negro/ in a blue
coat/ with a red lining/ in flight . . .

Hughson's stomach was the final cry and temper tantrum;
Hughson's stomach was Negroes rising like a mutiny of smoke;
Hughson's stomach was what wasn't yet—a nation—what it
would have prayed for. But right now it only had a God
and a bottomless hunger for a country.

A Six-Sided Cedar Coat

Hail doughty Ethiopian Chief!
Though ignominious Negro Thief!
This Black shall prop thy sinking name,
And damn thee to perpetual fame.
                    —*New York Journal* May 25, 1776

I.
Guerrilla Rangers in the Negro barracks
artisans from the Chesapeake, low-country
rice-swamp fugitives, all catching liberty's
virus once Lord Dunmore proclaimed eager-
ankled Negroes willing to desert the rebel standard
and defend his majesty, free: to be clenched

in war's fist; to flock to this belligerent
metropolis; to obey orders in war's disorder.
A loyalist is a patriot's (slave) traitor; a treason
of field hands behind British lines. Bondmen
might have been torn that charred September
when a quarter of New York was torched
and gagged on its own ashes

II.
Crouched near a chandlery, Frog Hall
or the tea pump, one dark loyalist could
have been Pompey Lamb, Inchu Moore
Bristol Budd or Salem Poor
                              He was
dead before the Treaty of Paris, where
Washington—then more Mount Vernon
mastermind than Yorktown's presented
arms—coveted the audacious and filched.
Article 7's fugitive flesh

                        Surely
dead before Patriots stamped their
new world in the *New World*

                        Definitely
gone when Black Pioneers greased
the Battery's flagpole. Union Jack
still rippling—blasphemous shad
                on the salty waterfront

                        Undoubtedly
dead, once the British surrendered
and evacuated blacks who'd enlisted
helping them board a *Book of Negroes*—
brigantines with dog-eared spinnakers
setting sail from Bowling Green. Three
thousand free: each individual a chapter
longing to be published in another country

III.
But whoever *he* was, having not embarked
now rots amongst the coffinless of Kalk
Hook Farm. Late, hilly land. Men stricken
with smallpox but without kith or kin
to buckle timber and bury them. Copper
coins atop eye sockets weight them
closed. These lids now glint. One

of the slung and forsaken has a winding-
sheet. And from a *long-gone* long coat
insignias of anchor and rope on
nine buttons. Collar to buckle.
Gilded and pewter. All befitting
a British sailor yet interred
with him. Six feet tall. Forty
never saw this Negro buried
without a six-sided cedar coat
to button his bones so the earth
will have little problem undressing him.

Feet-Me-Downs

No left or right at first, those lasts
had no suchness, no scuffed
disposition from earth worker's
steps and dictated stops. No his shoes
got their essence from echoing
his bunions and corns; got part

of their stamp from sweat snap
and juba stomp. No lining, hard
leather, unblackened, untanned
hobnailed, loose pegs, perforated
gnawed through bottom and welt.
Built to both blister and last: but

leather is dear and life cheap.
Once their owner's work had
been done—corpse stiff, supine
as a chucked shoe—his Nigger
Brogans was inched off.
Calloused soles of ashen

feet; wooden soles of run down
mules. Cleaved. Memories; miles—
both gimp *and* dash. Often sun-
baked but when soaked those withered
uppers doubled as rain's poxy, peripatetic
ladles. But no moseying to the bone-

yard, no skyward toes snug in a crypt
of hide and pine. Brogans cost too
much not to soldier on and stay bereft
of a Negro's breathing. Hence, un-
acquainted ankles were quickly made
to make their acquaintance to order

stiff wooden soles to apple picking
and fresh wooden floors. Those brogans
would goad and nick meek pinky toes
then need time-taking to inculcate as well
as be shaped by the devalued gallop, must
and heft of yet another trodden Negro body.

Kith

There's truth to the notion friends
can start to resemble each other.
That's what happened to Hughson

    and Caesar hung side by side
    since that spring's midriff. Both
    men mere ooze and reek: the earth

puckered and indifferent beneath them.
Hughson's hands blanched: chalky face
and feet supposedly turned black. His beard

    the hair on his neck wooled
    up. Nose flattened, aimless
    as a stain: nostrils sloughed

hollowed out. Mouth widened.
Lips thickened, baked—a halved
potato. Chalky skin sparkled darker

    than inky Caesar's. His Monmouth cap
    made it difficult to say whether his
    hair clenched and clenched like Caesar's

Those few months dangling snuffed
his whiteness and Hughson supposedly
mirrored Caesar's melanin. Caucasian no

mere accomplice but next of kin—or
at least first cousin—of Caesar's features.
And in life, the soles of Caesar's feet

his palms and teeth had always wanted to meet
Hughson's whiteness partway. As a cinched
pendulum, Caesar's effort continued:

his nose had pinched—a plank;
his lips turned to chapped wires.
And his flesh?   *Purified*

of sin while being peeled in the sun

BONEYARNS

Talking to the Bones:

What of your face?
A bullet is blunt as a comment

Your wrist?
Witness my resistance

How so?
The wrist twisted: cracked cloud under my skin

Who put the ball beneath your rib?
A musket seeking flesh
that only wanted freedom

Who buried you above an old man's bones?
Shallower the grave: less gristle
between here and heaven

But why only a right rib cage?
What we leave the earth
when we leave this earth
is not ours to say

Talking to the Bones: Another Columbia University Victim

What of the way of your demise?
This box—death's wooden bondage

Were you buried in a coffin?
No matter. This colony's a coffin with shores instead of sides

What of these students of physics?
I've heard when a body's scooped
chocolate coffins are 'natomy class coffers

But their behavior?
They stole what had already been
stolen. For us white was never
wanted but constently wanton

Why unearth only at night?
Cause darkness don't inspect the devil's sweat

To the Bones: About the Beads: Talking

That clear glass bead with a clear green heart in your grave?

That ocean we could not see
when we was dragged across
is a drop we shrunk and shackled
It's now our glittering revenge

There's a bead in the ground near what would have been your left ear—its lobe

Like all flesh, my lobe
(a bead I would
tickle and tug) agreed
to the earth's demands

Would this bead have clutched your hair?

Hair like skin also jilted
my bones, so that bead was left
nothing to cling to

What about the grey beads with eight facets?

Some beads got many sides.
Like stories. 'Spec'lly the ones
that are hard to hear . . . May I
ask you something?

I'm all ears

What is what you call wax for?

An ear's bodyguard to stop entry and injury

Well that bead you spotted
close to what once was
my ear, thought of wax
as a skull's soil as sound's
sugar: bitter and caked

To the Bones: About the Beads: Talking

On your right wrist, why the bracelet of turquoise and yellow glass beads?

After the pound and soak of Master's
   nankeen breeches I would find myself
inching on dawn in his damp cellar.
   kneeling. My swole hands gloved in foam

I'm confused

That bracelet: cruel jewelry or may-
   be just a blue and yellow warning
if the hand I favored bent too far back

Your bracelet puts me in mind of a cute shackle

What?

Pardon me

See where back of my hand
   below my pinky meets
my wrist? That peeking
   bone pressing against
my bracelet was once
   a shy, bent-on-hiding, bead

To the Bones: About the Beads: Talking

The 100-plus waist beads strung around your midriff?

They was always hidden under the cast-off
clothes the Mrs. had me wear: stained
linsey aprons. tattered petticoats. There
something close to home worked my hips

150 beads in the entire cemetery. 110 were yours

My body somebody: an elder here.
A chief's child: somewhere—else: where?

On that strand of waist beads, there were seven cowrie shells. Why?

I've heard seven seas bully
the earth. I met one. three
months. brief-like. wasn't pleasant.

Tell me more

My every breath—its fleshy
belonging to—reeled here.
naked. save these beads
that circled my left thigh
bounced off my hips
                    Imagine
                            feeling like you're carrying a country around your waist?

A nation of blue beads, huh?

Or maybe just clinched echoes of that ocean. small
reminders of a white man's transatlantic tantrum

Talking to the Bones

Of the nine Akan beads in the entire cemetery, eight yellow beads were around a two-month old's neck.

    Again. It's a story of water: its body/our bodies. That baby's
    jewelry an omen drifting across the ocean. Every white cap a stitch
    in what would turn out to be that child's last, gasping fabric

So small, seems she was buried in a wig box. But she was laid to rest with an elder

    Thank goodness her infant coffin tucked in
a grown man's
      grave. Grandfather and grandchild? Niece? Uncle?

Talking to the Teeth

Now you are one with a skull: its white hush
    But sometimes a mouth was a hot leaking
    cottage we was all forced to live in

Front tooth, why were you whittled to an enamel fang?
    Animal fang? What animal?

*Not animal. **Enamel.** Teeth ingredients. like what you been reduced to: bone*
    When she giggled. chewed or smiled some knew
    I might be the one thing she clung to from home

In the children's graves, their teeth were almost always gone
    Cause they was the here-born. The start
    life. The too-often sugar and corn suppers

In the back of your mouth, one of you looks like a peg.
    Death picks everything clean. Here now
    skinned, stripped, lips can no longer
    hush us—way a lid might muffle
    a pot of cornmeal mush.

And, you, tooth, shaped like an hourglass?
    A tooth occasionally tells a skull's time: means I was
    born and adorned before this unwelcoming earth

Talking to the Bones: Talking

Had you abandoned baby talk?
we was the unwelcomed welcome

Why were over half of you under two?
our end here in this unkind earth

Had you moved beyond mother's milk?
mouths without nipples just sob and wander

Talking to the Bones: Talking

What harbors the pain?
                        My neck a buckling dock

Why is your forearm where your shin should be?
                    Each bone should have its own uh-uh

What had the aches attended?
                        We the ones of two soils/two souls:
Coromantee; the filthy gleam of Amsterdam or York

Why?
            Here we reached old bones
            because we grew up back home.
            There we ate untroubled suppers
            for the gizzard and the spirit

I see
First breath Akan   Last beat New Amsterdam

Talking to the Bones: Talking

Why bury the pate facing west?
Then setting sun only nicks the sockets

That first snow?
White tears drifting
                                    from the whites
of the sky's puffy eyes

What type of toil did you do?
Work. until the bones were wrinkled by song

Why the halfpence on your eyes?
Think full moon: throb
                                    of a distant drum
that once played you

What was it like to have graves without names?
Come again?

JUPITER & WHEATLEY'S SUITE

After Jupiter Hammon and Phillis Wheatley.
Hammon, of Queens Village, New York,
was the first published Negro poet in the colonies.
Wheatley was the first Negro to publish an entire book.

Scribble: Jupiter Hammon

Chattel can be an entire planet: a first name
hailing from outer space. Jupiter's parents
beckoned by the original Lloyd ship-
ment. Father Obadiah—good fortune

onyx prophet :: an old testament—taught
to read and write. Jupiter: 1711 addition
to the Lloyds—and Obadiah—schooled in
more than the three "r's" while romping

the Horse Neck Manor House. Given
the scribble gift. To the kids: "Brother
Jupiter." Brother Jupiter!? Yet his breath
always buttoned to someone: first

a father then his
son lastly to a great-
grand. Still *Jup's* was
an independent orchard. He could

rise an hour after
ring-bell. Decked
in linen homespun, he
gilded frames with gold

leaf; manned the corncrib and smoke
house; counted sterling from ten-
ant farm quitrent, plus the sale
of the good book. needles. Beholden

to no one—mostly—but some
times as house servant, his
was the on-call, kiss-close
contact with Master's family.

Still. never freed. Sixteen years
before a nation congealed Christmas
1760, he for the first time skirted a right
jagged edge: "An Evening Prayer.

Salvation by Christ with Penitential Cries:
Composed by Jupiter Hammon, a Negro
belonging to Mr. Lloyd of Queen's Village."
A poem. A broadside published before

the Republic. The Negro's first
printed offense in English while Jupiter
fidgeted under the supple
and galactic shadow of suffering.

Deem Me: Piter/Pater

(in the imagined voice of Jupiter Hammon)

I.
Deem me distant. *Ju*piter.
"*Ju*/Zeus." Shared root.
Piter of Latin's *pater* :: father

Piter/Pater: Zeus the father.
Pitter-patter. Make sound
light. rapid. repeat. Neptune/

Poseidon. Dis/Pluto. My siblings.
Hell and seas. Cosmic: our
parcels. Heaven: my realm

II.
But here on the bottom of America's
airy envelope, I'm just a wanderer
spinning yet held in this colonial
orbit, this gravitational pull, this
solar system: one of billions

III.
With his telescope glommed on-
to flickering mysteries if only Galileo
could have discovered me there
on the shores of his surname
(Nazareth tucked in the foothills)

between the Jordan and Mediterranean
where what I covet of anglers and God

where sudden calms and violent storms
of wind and wave are normal—like my surface
where there's a brick-red tempest 30,000
miles long. That infidel, that stellar dervish

IV.
Stars are the sky's twinkling preachers.
The firmament: Galilee's vertical sea.
Something my savior can walk upon.
If Galileo could prove things
helio—as a child I thought I
could pray to my Lord crack
the crust of my icy core

V.
Deep Space: mere sea where the splash
has vanished. Ganymede, Callisto—
my ardent moons: one a maiden.
Me: a heavenly body fettered

to this system: colonial, solar.
Yet I'm the largest planet
craw vast enough to hold
eight others—including

the one I'm on. But I lack
a solid surface. This is what
happens to a man who never
questions his servitude

VI.
Think of the orbit between an Oyster Bay Estate and New York
City as the orbit between Jupiter—me—and Mars. An asteroid belt.
Galactic scraps, the sky's parasites a surfeit of genesis and suffering
that brought me about thousands of millions of years ago

VII.
Snag in the fabric of space-time
Everywhere. Invisible. Baffling.
I neither absorb admit nor reflect.
Dark matter. 95% of everything.

Stand before me. Encourage your eyes
to adapt. In just minutes you'll
glimpse heaven: the cosmos:
its snarling displaced dark majority

Tinged

Carted to Hartford during the Revolution
    Jupiter published another poem: "An Address
to Miss Phillis Wheatley;" she more slave
    than he for she minded her master's name.
Hammon: his and his alone. He likely

addressed her because of their common
bond—the word—or common bond-
age—to masters. Still, Connecticut was
an Episcopal wedge between New York
and Massachusetts. But war brought *Jup*

and Phillis closer. And he, like his masters,
    was certainly tinged by New England's
religious revivals. Envision him owned
    and composed while composing:
each syllable a religion. His quill—

no matter how holy—penning
a Negro's illegal ink while he balked
at the heretic in Wheatley's verse.
But not one of his poems fingered
the Lloyds' slaving and piety.

With Phillis, Bible verses
    plumped his every verse, him
brandishing grammatical shackles
    far from the cankered chains that
bound his father in the fetid hold

of a Guineaman's hold. *Jup*: blind
to the dainty manacles that hamstrung
tetrameter and trimeter flights. "Heav'nly,
ev'ry, 'tis and 'twill; might'st, advis'd,
o'er, and 'twere." How *e* endures

erasure—at times *v* or *i* —all forsaken
    for a syllable's sake. *For this cottage*
of clay . . . touched by . . . redeeming . . . grace
    conned from . . . heathen shores . . . by
the Lord's shepherd.

      There's resignation knowing
life is equal parts prose and poetry
is as disposed to drudge as lyric.

An Almost Audience
(for *Phillis* Wheatley)

Of Senegambia and seven, she should have been of the not-to be-taken,
the not-high price for a not-prime boy's a girl of the unsuitable labor—
birth not work—and that years away. (The captured: their spirits: ships
sinking inside them.) But there could have been a rising up: so she was of
the constant watch, the on your guard, the danced-on-deck, the Captain
Gwinn and merchant Fitch, the sterling purchase. Haunches, flanks
slicked and oiled before the shore; sold then resold in Boston Harbor.
Profit, barter and harvest/barter, harvest and profit; trinkets slaves and
salt cod/salt cod trinkets and slaves

Bought then brought on the Middle Passage but would one day read
passages of her work in London. Neither stowage cash crop nor export—
bidden thought garnering an almost-audience with George III, an actual
one with Washington. For on a ship, your prayer is to reach as well as
return

She who'd been named for the schooner that brought her to Boston.
Three months crumpled in the hull: like being trapped in a capsized
Macaw's rank beak. The gulfweed, the squawk the whistle, the mimic
of the ocean's moods or inhuman moans. (That *un*equilateral tragic
triangle) She remembered parrots in savannah oil palms: charcoal heads,
constant chatter, pearl millet gleaming in their beaks. Boston worthies
called her parrot—inky mimic

But little of that life in her tutored lines: merchant's servant, sickly
infants, more words but no means to publish them. A cooped husband—
free-black grocer who'd set penury on a feeble table. *Poems on Subjects
Religious and Moral*: hell is an elegy one never finishes

In her eye's leaking northern light, she might have recalled Horace, declension, Homer and Greek, fame's tentative shimmer; homilies on Washington and Milk at the Old South Meeting House. Or though emancipated, she might have thought of escape, to "join the angelic train" embarking on the ship listing slipshod and backwards through her name: *Phillis*

Sable Marginalia

At this hour of unlettered clocks
                              —Yusef Komunyakaa

At 20, Phillis produced
   an entire book. (In
the preface and after
   a court of authorship, Boston
worthies—Chauncy, Erving
   and Hancock—attested
she'd penned each syllables'

ink and halt.) She who

   had the first book published
by a Negro in the New
   World but whose final
days were spent shriveling
   as a scullery maid
in a tumble-
   down boardinghouse.

FREEDOM SUITE

Coating: *Warwick*

Gray and against the weather, my great
coat—open, soft—like the cover
of a wool book. Underneath: my waist
-coat (only two pages I can read)

Balled in one of them pockets:
the difficult print: a supposed-to-say
bill of sale: proof 'bout how I bought
back what had never been sold. Myself

Here exposed to the elements: rickety

slush pawing at my ankle. Free—
but still lugging a curfew. After
dark, so they can spot a welt on
my cheek but still not see me, I clutch

a lantern—a second head: high
neckless and blank. Inside its
panes of shaved bone, the sun:
cornered, blazing (caged)

Long in That Late-Afternoon Light: *Bukay*

I want to give Suley another name
maybe not hers but not her master's.
'Scort her to charade clubs. Airs.
Fin'ries. No more moldy kerchiefs
roofing her 'do or baize aprons that feel
welcome as felt when I'm smuggling

           Sunday smooches. She the apple
           of my black eye. More'n two years
           now been figuring a way to buy
           her bondage and sniff what I don't
           ever has to consider: freedom.
           A given. It's mine. But no

matter if it's ten months at sea
or two on land huddlin' rags
there's a shadow won't let me
be: out front or following at times.
It's mine and not mine—long
in that late-afternoon light

           Swells on a wave's salty shoulders;
           withering on a ship's buckled deck;
           snaps in a wrinkled snowdrift.
           This here shadow even shadows
           me at night. Got to be Suley stitched
           to me. Her right hand balled inching

up inching down. head low. Cain't
say if it's focused, heartsick or both.
But it's sewing a mantua: them
gowns that flow like lampshades
wit' pleats. Shades that part-ways
dim the don't-you-look light

of a white woman's legs. Suley
and me had a Negro union. But she's
wantin' a legal one, wants me take
her trembling hand in marriage;
so I can take more than just her
shadow wherever and whenever I go.

Full Out: *Richard*

Not Dicky Boy or Rich. Richard.
That's what I go by now. Richard.
Smith. My names—not odd

      enough to notice. Blend in. Sound
      like my freedom as I straddle up
      John Street and hear my name—full

out from someone's mouth near
the clapboard Methodist. Decent
white folk Sunday there. Recognizin'

      the name caller, I tip my hat and head
      as if I'm spilling my thinking, the way
      a tippler might spill a drink. Some my wool—

plaited, tied with dried eel—glancing off
my right ear like a tipsy whisper: some
precious secret that ain't easy in its keepin'

Kin: *Quack*

I been told there's more letters between
        the "F" in *free* and the "N" in *Negro*

than between the "N" in *Negro* and the "S"
        in *slave* in they word house. So *slave*

and *Negro* almost next of kin.
"Cinomims," I believes they word

        for it. But *free* comes up short in 'ticular
ways. For starters, one less letter—I was told

        Negro and *slave* got a equal number. Yep.
Negro and *free*: they's got no relations.

STOCKS AND BONDAGE
Wall Street

(Two Centuries/Three Parts)

A. Construction

Whether rampart or Walloon

                     Bulwark or Belgian Pilgrim

De Waal or *Wal Straat*

                  the u n s e t t l e d erected that

doubled palisade and walk

               way, that nubbly wooden fence;

the u n s e t t l e d constructed the northern

                  edge of the Dutch interruption.

To protect whites from the *Red*

                 and other whites blacks built

an earthen wall where a street

               is named for what a squint can

no longer crush nor a dawdler's

              knuckle mull: the *wall* on Wall Street.

B. Auction: Hell's Unbidden Hello

The stench smashed against every dock
-side nostril: sweat's unanswered
dread, cruelty's cheap perfume.
That reek proclaimed the unseen
but surely limping Guineaman

a seasick fist, balled, faltering
in the Atlantic, harboring
three months of the West
African terror. The squinting
whys in those abducted eyes:

what the ocean failed to answer: hell's
first hello. A street nudged by the East
River. Rowboats. Oars. Pier 17. The Old
Slip. Where Wall met Water Street. Pacing
cobbles, a white gentleman—nothing

but tummy and muttonchops—would mount
a platform, hoist a gavel, and fifty Africans
would lumber from the hold up six
dank steps, huddling under a wooden
roof, where, at the foot of this city, lazing

beneath the forked shadow of a dragon
beam, Indians and the colony's long-since
slaves were sent to seek new ways to scoop
a shilling and sweat; were rented hired or let
out by the day or week. Uneyed. Mobile.

Downtime. Cozy. But the huddled: *"FOR
SALE* young strapping *BUCK* along with
a *NEGRO WENCH*. Inquire at 57 Jane-
way Lane." Bought. Traded. Auctioned.
Off: to till and build/to chore and cook.

In and around this *unsouthern* structure, this
New England gazebo—looming—buyers
circled, eyed ballooning chests, smalls of backs
scoops in flanks. Preparing for a nearly naked sale
a white middle and index finger nose along

a brow's frightened horizon. Beads of
sweat—signal and gift—brought to that
buyer's tongue. Smack: a colony's first taste
of a continent. Not salty, hence not sick: an African
sold along with a knob of *un*sifted cereal grass

C. Buttonwood Agreement

Structured compensation. Standardized commission. Broker Dealer Trader Speculator. Highest bidder. Buy. Sell. Shares. Bonds. Financial. Clients. Transaction. Certificate. Merchants. Securities.

Buttonballs cling to twigs through winter only to find earth's footing come spring

Intermediary/short-term/contract/profit/purchase/negotiate/bargain/distribute. Fluctuate and Hope. Regulate and Market. Flutter. Fee. Rate. Floor commission. Wall and Water. Yet again.

Two dozen men fettered by preference—and longing to be bound by idea institution and ink—convene at a tree. Its crown turns the heaven's brittle; the sky's blue scattered. Shade: an incidental gift. A single quill. The shaft: hollow monastery of wetness. Tips of fingers pinching a feather: its annual shadow shedding on the back of a signer's hand. flight=sky; flow=ink. feather: bind them both. Heel first: each hand crosses the document's continent. Ink::

thought's blood:: (clotting)

At the foot of 68 Wall an agreement reached under a buttonwood tree. Above those signers' heads, a leaf beetle inching across and conquering an olive continent.

Mid-spring is an illness: sticky buds in a petiole's sleeve; heartwood: dim and dense; little give for a trunk coming into its own within the wood's secret churning world. A chunk of piebald bark sloughs. Seed-ball hair cranky in his throat: a man coughs. cough. A leaf's coat stripped: it's itch seeking refuge in the crow's-feet of some

of the signers' eyes.

That nagging Antebellum shadow adorns shipping, cotton and insurance, covering companies in the trade: black and bought on credit

VIII

An Honorable Harvest

                                   Let us interrupt ourselves slowly because
                                   nearly half of us burn the bread and
                                   breath of our fettered brethren. Slave-
                                   holders are we: James, Duane, Johns—

Jay and Lamb—and Alexander
Hamilton. More than one of two
Manumission Society members traffic
in the epidermis of others.
                         Shout it down

                                   in The South, as a trade, as an idea
                                   or on the islands. But (y)ours is milder.
                                   Let the suffering slide when and if
                                   or if and when there's an honorable

harvest. Yet somehow hypocrisy's
crop crops up in (y)our own colony

Ashley and New Amsterdam

New York:

second only

       to the city of Cooper, Ashley
       and indigo mid-April azaleas
       Sumter and rice;

second only

       to a land's constricted neck:
       a peninsula and its avowed
                 acres;

second only

       to a way of life
       cinched on three
       sides by liquid. 750
       miles and a *supposed*

                    world

                        away

After/thought/After/life

Once a spotless water source, the Fresh
    Water Pond became a British
privy, a dump, a lie: *fresh water*;
    became a skirmish between shilling
and spirit, because, even swampy

    wan, this lakelet: sacred to the for-
saken. Here of marsh and Potter's
    House, of windmill and bluff,
the upstanding—Recine & Rips Tan
    Yard for one—hedged and desecrated

those who were often down-
    trodden and, at the Grounds, down-
hearted. Pinched and shifted a century-
    old cemetery: its north south and east.
Rude blooming industry pawed

    at the Collect's shores. Spirits ruthlessly
polluted when colonists whisked
    what the city no longer wanted—
cow horns and slaughterhouse
    chuck—to the outskirts beyond

the palisades Africans constructed
    past another self-inflicted skirt;
dumped it along with pitched hides
    and clay waste. Muddy debris—parch
-ment of the pond—mixed ballooned

fifteen feet, as if a wart had plumped
and spread atop the filthy Collect. Its
small body an African silhouette: wet.
reflected. Kalk Hook Farm, Van Borsum
Patent—private property that skirted

the burial ground. African spirit space
low-lying ravine, seven potent acres where
tanneries minced a century, backfilling
the Negroes' graves: as if these industries
deemed the African afterlife, merely the earth's

afterthought

Breath's Breath: *Japhet*

When I'm cursing them tanners under
my breath's breath, I speak *Yankeyfied*
Negro English. Gathered bit of limping
French and Spanish on a voyage

to *Cadiz*; anchor jarring *Caleta's*
sleepy waters. Beach pinched
between two castles. Actually
city lil' more'n a spit:

twisting alleys, a square, some
tower called *Tavira*. Designs
'round its windows: hoot owl
face: rust-colored eyebrows

upturned moustache. But New
York's tanners' yards always
loud makings and bold odors
right there in the burial ground—

our Negro frontier where mosquitoes
serve malaria's *fevery* meal during
the two months my sea legs would sink.
But who am I—rag picker; sailor; there-

and-here day laborer between Mulberry
and Orange. Still I'm ekin' something out
of winter: a living from its hard margins
where I gather chucked cloth and leavings:

hog hocks and corn sheaves. Right
about now could use Cedar Street Tavern:
a nip of spirit'us liquor, a shot of liquid
forgetting, shatterin' in the gulch of my throat

A Clockwise Tizzy

Linen to swaddle her in maybe
shroud. Brass pins stiff straight:
supportive rigor mortis. A coffin: hex-

agonal, cedar. Beads and schist pepper
her remains. Conjure bundle broken
stoneware, blue spiral in the bowl's

heart. Crolius-Remmey kiln
furniture. Blue: land of the
ancestors. Say *underwater*

say *Kongo cosmogram* say *cross-
roads*. On her coffin's lid, this
cracked vessel: small talk between

the living and the dead. Their law insists: light;
night—West Africa's credo. Head headed
west. pate indifferent to the Atlantic.

chin braced for the sun's untidy rising. If
the living could build an almshouse of sorrow
they would circle this socked earth: this yawning

soil, this plot. A shriek a wail a drum bludgeoned
anchoring a clockwise tizzy. Yet those who
forced enslaved and free mourners beyond

the city's sullen edges could not believe death
would be the sole reason for the Negro
clump. There had to be another plot—

an ebon about to be—fixed on an oppressor's death
while honoring a loved one's. Hence no more
than a dozen Africans are ever allowed to help

the dearly departed depart. Still, over weeping
cedar, they pass a suckling's pudge:
its newborn shadow a pressing matter

between innocence and the dogma of bone

First and Final

Coffin for his negro boy coffin
      for his negro girl coffin for

his negro child black coffin
      for a negro child coffin

for Jane a negro coffin for Mo[lly?]
      a negro coffin for his negro

woman coffin for a negro
      woman coffin for negro

woman with screws black
      coffin for his negro woman

rozind with screws a large coffin
      for his negro coffin for his

negro man rough coffin
      for Joseph Castins negro:

here, the sole African with a first
      and last name, where omega

and alpha is merely death's
      alphabet::bookends

of a first and final breath

Talking to the Bones

Had you made Joshua Delaplaine's acquaintance, Mr. Castins?
Death: a sad cabinet is it not?

Joseph, when did Delaplaine put you in his account book?
My account: with God

*How did you die with a given **and** surname?*
The first shall have a last and the last shall have a first

Nail and Pine

Somewhere warps a coffin with your first
and sur—Joseph Castins. It's rumored

slaveowner Caleb Lawrence gave it to
Joshua Delaplaine who likely inquired

as had not happened with other Negroes
swaddled with nail and pine: surely not

for the dozen others Joshua had carved
coffins for. Either Delaplaine cared less

to ask or masters cared little to mention
their expired Negroes' names. Of the dozen

others, three had one. All women. Each first:
Mo[lly?] rozind and Jane. Yours the one first

and last of over 400. Two names: with as many
letters as there are colonies on a saw-toothed coast.

Extra letters that could have afforded you another
life. July Seventeen Fifty-Five: proof in a cabinet-

maker's account book. Between the last letter
of your first name and the first letter of your

last name: space: an unetched headstone: dead
speechless tooth. White men might have called you

Mr. Castins in life or only murmured that
designation after your demise—yet to be

known in life offers no escape from death.
Sorrow might have driven Caleb Lawrence

to boldly raise you up as death inevitably
let you down. For we have the name Joseph

Castins but no coffin to be found: this entry
on a page without an entry
                                    in the earth

This Is Sorcery

I. *Incantation*

Suck the sun from a knuckle
then the ichor from a pinky
powder the elbow's low tide

the puddle of the knee, the shoulder's
tines, the spatterdash and linen kerchief;
cuddle burial ground earth soil

of the been-done gone. Let bone
and absence agitate. This spirit-
filled *minkisi* will shield

the brethren from bullets:
"Go," free Peter the Doctor,
the *nganga*, insists.

II. *Invitation*

We know where this approaching night
  must bloom, where feces and piss flower
    where noses won't invite themselves. Peter
      the Baker's outhouse, we'll meet: 2 a.m.
        The orchard on Maiden Lane, 23
          wait: *Quito, Quack, Quash,* Andries'
            Peter—the porter—Roosevelt's Tom

Adolph's *Amba*: Sarah, Abigail, maybe Lilly;
   Sarah, Lilly maybe Abby; Lilly, Abby maybe
      Sarah . . . maybe; maybe; maybe, maybe . . . Sarah
         Abigail and/or Lilly; Sarah, Lilly and/or
            Abby; Lilly, Abby and/or Sarah . . . and
               /or; and/or; and/or . . . this Akan and English
                  hodgepodge

But here a flower that will call itself fire—
petals not of April but flame—when Van
Tilburg's *Cuffee* and his Spanish Juan set
shit ablaze. Sepals, hot, spied by nearly 50
arms armed with flintlocks and half-basket hilts.

With houses shoulder to shoulder
wood is a deep wound no able-bodied
bucket brigade can stanch. *Paw*
Paw and a first people's Spanish trio
knew outhouse flames would draw
townsfolk out who dreaded what fire might
do but neither feared nor knew the statute

            and lurk of musket and axe of right arms held
               tardy and high as 11 o'clock. Peter—not the doctor
            but the porter—takes a dagger to Joris. Tom's
         shot makes of Andries' chest a bloody blossom.
         (Lead: never a well-intentioned metal.) All
      these arms driven into nine, unsuspecting
   whites rushing headlong to light into this fire . . .

III. *Benediction*

      All rise in this court of slaughter! Testify to New York's first slave

revolt, to six who took their lives seriously

      enough to kill themselves

      to April and owners

deposed against their own property, to guilt

      ensconced in a snarl and the conscience of a palm withered by revenge

I. Which/One: 1712 Slave Revolt

Abigail? Sarah? Equally rebels. But which

one womb, nearly nine months, 200-

bone home? Which one

want to usher to this ugly, life?

(A black lilac hoping to bloom in the family way)

Which old soul for newborn, which

one six-week teeth, which

nearly-milk, belly swell? Which one

raise hell to raise

child free?

Which one her one

hope to see April shower but won't

see May flower? (see, she never cottoned to the long hour) Which

long-since maiden lying

in wait: Maiden Lane, half-basket hilt

                    poised undaunted

before urine and shit. Sugar
                         maple: which one

                                             crouched near its long-winged seeds

and sweet, eventual sap, which one

                                        nurturing fetus and fire in her belly

planning to birth
                               murder? Which one

blood stopped: (menses) months before
                                              she made colonial blood flow?

See, she done "playing the lady" for a bit less back-break and a little more cornmeal

                          Which one struck flint to gunpowder?

Which one bone girdle? Which

                              one 4-month feel it—the quickening—which one

sensed baby-leg move, palm

                        blossom, tiny fingers fist? Which one look

down as something somersaults in her stomach?

Which one fetus scoop, atlas for embryo

delivery date globed between darkened nipple and hip
                                        sanguine between cocked and shot?

Which one tender, nine-moon knot? What

                            the etymology of Sarah of Abigail

of air? Which father's joy? What prophetess?

                            Which Genesis? What Testament? Where

Africa in these appellations? Which

                            Gysbert? Which Stophell? Which

Vaninburgh? Which Pels? Witch

                            doctor. Peter? Which root doctor?
Morning sickness

            midwife's *knowery*, when? When
                                        to administer black haw or blue

cohosh? In the lying-in room? How long

                            to decompose this inky composition
for this alphabet to utterly

flesh itself out? Which one—

like her body eventually—had her   suspended?

                                      sentence   Which one

                    hid beside the same kind

of wood she'll hang from? Hard.

                                      Which will you give leave to
give birth only to turn around

                              and take her life? Why? Tell me

which one will be for months or days

                              or weeks a scorned warning—festooned

in a braided chain—meant to halt the dim

                                      ideas of the othered *others*? Aye, which

          gibbet will be choked

                              up, stunned, unable to shed this

teeming black teardrop?

II. Which, Too/Split Flash: *Break*

In a pinched and dank corner cell at the corner
of Wall and Broad, without
interrogation or constitution, beneath rulings and arches: four dials on a clock,
beneath arguments and archives: petit juries and supreme court, beneath criers
and bailiffs: peals and flutters, beneath bells and constables and birds and cupolas,
beneath perches and deputies: whipping posts and small talk, beneath windows
and guilt: wainscot and lawyers, beneath deep thought and bench wigs: warrants
and decorum, beneath two floors and black robes: conviction and handwringing
beneath plaintiffs and gavels: punishment and appeal, beneath charge and
indictment a hung head's arrest, beneath a trial and its rumors before acquittal
and pardon there's a case and its verdict before a judge and one's peers, beneath
sentences and pillory, evidence and stairwells, between wrongdoing and wrong
done and who's right and what's wrong:: The City Hall dungeon, where in darkness
lies a woman with child. So, no question of where labor. But when labor/what
labor—slave? slave—who labor even in labor. Sarah? Abigail? Which is dying to lie
on her left side—*shackled to staples with staples affixed to history: stone slaves once
quarried to build a wall boiled down to a street.* Which one's water break? Which
one gush or trickle: damp to the woolsey, sweet to the nose? How hard? When
tender? Abdomen. When hard? How tender? Uterus. Ache—how dull? *Shackled
to the . . . stapled to the . . . bolted to the agony: stone slaves once used to build . . .*
pressure: pelvis: how long? When is during between? What is between (en) during?
The stench of a Necessary tub? Contractions? Waves: water's pushy guests. 45
seconds (or so). Which one's still talking? Maybe one . . . *shackled to the . . . stapled
to the . . . bolted to the . . . memory: stone slaves once used . . .* Maybe 15 minutes later.
Maybe one. Maybe a minute (or) two later. or half a minute longer. stretch marks.
silence. Which one's stomach's a punch? Clenched. A fist. Breathe. Into the lower
back, into the ache. Knowing you got not even a sip of say-so over your captors'
shoe music composed on the floor above you *shackled to the . . . stapled to the . . .
bolted to these echoes*

III. Sundered

Stooping. whips. gruel. dirt for sustenance. Sarah?
Abigail? Which rebel kept alive, esteemed: until
she delivered her dark cargo? Which woman over
worked what child underweight? Which fruit—its
purchased womb—now ripened? Which one had longed
to own this approaching moment having never possessed
herself? still. she gave birth. A stillbirth? No. Which
umbilical? Which placenta? A veil over the infant's face?
Which woman, which *one* will only have an instant—skin
to skin—to bond in bondage. a moment to dilute her newborn's
tears, to offer a slim suckle? Sundered from her child's sobbing
there would be no wean in the fullness of time. no wet-nurse.
No. though she had authored her offspring, cooed its day name.
Some mothers are separated by sale. she by death; by hanging.
Will this child come to know beriberi and night blindness? Chores.
will there be for a three-year-old, chores? Toting? Plucking? When
will the death of its mother and a life of bondage dawn
                                        on this child like a bitter morn?

Talking to the Bones

But what of the North?

Master's doorknob:

        cotton boll.

'Neath my rag rug—

          his 'notty, gapped, strip-pine planks:

                      Tarboro plantation

Your pipe?

      Spirit

          is

            smoke

                plans on puffin'

                      myself

Day's end.

                           Work done.

Deceased beckoned   by chant

and drum   Masters—rare

participants—   secure

in their   echoing

          ] absence [

for the Common Council limited

thickets of mourners to twelve

and the knot of goodbye to no later

than the sun's hunched farewell

BONEYARN NOTES

There are approximately 15,000 bodies in a nearly seven-acre area just outside the northern limit of what was Colonial/Early National Period New York City—known as the Negro Burial Ground in what is now Lower Manhattan. (From the seventeeth century to the 1830s, New York was 1.5 miles from its southern tip to its northern boundary, a mile across east to west.) Enslaved and free Negroes, as well as a small number of Native Americans and poor/indentured whites are interred in this cemetery. The National Park Service, along with Howard University and others, exhumed 419 of those bodies and established a national monument on the site of the Ted Weiss Federal Building. Because only one full name of an enslaved individual, Joseph Castins, is known to be buried in the slave cemetery, the archaeologists, anthropologists, and osteologists gave numbers to the bones and coffins they unearthed. The cemetery was used from approximately 1712–1795.

PRELUDE

Colonial Cemetery: One theory for the opening of the Negro Burial Ground was that the colonists allowed some Negroes to worship in churches such as New York's historic Trinity Church (1697–1795), but the white colonial congregants would not allow Negroes, enslaved or free, to be buried in the cemetery. In October 1697, Trinity Church issued a statement: "Ordered, that after the expiration of four weeks from the date hereof no Negroes be buried within the bounds and limits of the church yard of Trinity Church." The church had owned its land for only five months. The Negro Burial Ground was considered outside New York City's boundaries.

Assignment (Columbia University slave cemetery graverobbers): In 1788 there was a Doctor's Riot in New York City because Columbia University medical school students (some as young as fifteen) were exhuming bodies from the graves of poor whites. The graverobbers then exhumed bodies from the Negro Burial Ground. A young white male had been taunted by a medical school student who had dangled a limb out of a hospital window and joked that it belonged to the boy's mother. Unbeknownst to the medical student, the boy's mother had just died. The boy's father gathered a large number of working-class whites who attempted to assault and kill some of the Columbia medical students and their professors. Police and military had to be called out to protect the students. In the midst of this melee, free Negroes petitioned New York's Common Council (the local governing body, comparable to today's City Council) to, if not completely stop the graverobbing, at least treat the enslaved Negro bodies with dignity. The Council had been considering a "bone bill," legislation which would have stopped the graverobbing, but the bill had not passed up to that that point. Some information about the early history of Columbia University/Kings College can be found at History of Columbia University, https://en.wikipedia.org/wiki/History_of_Columbia_University.

Telling Time: This grave contained three coffins. The largest coffin contained an adult woman's body and within that coffin two much smaller coffins had two infants inside—one of the children not even a year old. The supposition is that the adult woman was the mother and these were her children, but scientists were not able to determine what caused their deaths or why they were seemingly buried at the same time.

SECTION I

Chimney Sweep Apprentice (enslaved teenager, New York, eighteenth century): Enslaved Negro boys (as well as young white males) were employed as chimney sweep apprentices, cleaning the flues of colonists' homes, who often waited until the winter holidays for the service. The work was perilous and started before dawn. Often the chimney sweep—the boys' "boss"—was a grown Negro male who might also have been enslaved. The boys could be as young as five years old because they had to be small enough to fit into the flue. Boys sometimes got stuck in there and died; some came down with scrotal "chimney sweep" cancer. The term "light a fire under him" came from other boys lighting a match and putting it at the heels of a boy who refused to climb higher into a chimney. The boys' skeletal structures (limbs and spines) frequently became deformed from malnutrition as well as the unnatural positions the boys assumed in the chimneys. The boys carried soot bags which were too heavy for their young bodies and which also deformed their backs.

Mercy (New York City slave revolt): In 1712, a group of twenty-four enslaved Negroes, "Spanish Indians," and some Native Americans plotted to set fire to a baker's, Peter Van Tilburg's, outhouse hoping it would draw out white colonists to extinguish the fire. Using muskets, hatchets, swords, and knives, the conspirators then planned to murder the colonists who tried to put out the blaze. The conspirators eventually aimed to kill all the colonists and also hoped other enslaved people would join in their effort, but most of the conspirators—and many others who might not have been involved—were captured, tried, and executed. A slave named Claus, who likely had not participated in the revolt, was swept up in the hysteria and was tried; his punishment was to be "broken on the wheel" until death. The Commons would be the equivalent of the New York's City Hall area.

Kip was a street in lower Manhattan.

Fire was extremely dangerous in colonial New York because of all of the City's wooden structures.

The Thomas Jefferson epigraph comes from his 1784 essay collection *Notes on the State of Virginia* (Query XVIII: Manners, 1781) and captures his thoughts about what "retribution/justice" might be visited from "upon high" on the United States of America for the cruel institution of slavery.

Knuckles of Smoke: *Peggy* (enslaved cook, 1780s): Unlike the majority of enslaved individuals in the South, almost all those enslaved in New York—and New England generally—lived in their masters' houses, often in either the cellars or attics. The cellars frequently doubled as the cooking areas, so they could be unduly hot. The grueling work of moving heavy pots caused spinal damage in many enslaved women.

Whistlelo (A free Negro living in an attic with two enslaved Negroes, 1790s): Most free Negroes also lived in the houses of whites with other enslaved individuals in either an attic or cellar. Although free, these Negroes had little of the rights of a white male colonist. They could not vote, testify in court, or serve on a jury, especially in a case against a white person. There were also codes such as curfews. No more than three Negroes could congregate at any time during the day or make noise (such as laughing). Violations could result in whipping. These strictures affected Native American slaves as well.

Negro Chimney Sweep (beyond the flue: enslaved New York chimney sweep apprentice, nineteenth century): The blanket the chimney sweeps used to collect filth from the chimneys was also the same blanket they slept in. They used a scraper to loosen the tar and residue in the flue and a brush to knock it off. A sweep cap was worn in the flue to keep the tar and other materials such as creosote out of their eyes, mouths, and nostrils. In the wee hours, the often-malnourished apprentices walked the streets bellowing "Sweep-O, Sweep-Sweep." That call alerted interested homeowners to the fact that the apprentices were available to work. The Christmas holidays were the high season.

Franklin stove: metal heating stove, resembling an open fireplace.

Puffback: puffs of smoke that brought soot particles into a house. Combustion caused a boom, and big vibrations shook loose accumulated soot and an oily, sticky film with a strong smell. Misfiring of puffback gases trapped in stoves' fireboxes could send soot throughout a house.

The boys endured sudden shifts from the frigid winter temperatures to the hot chimneys. Some of the collected soot was sold to farmers as fertilizer. Many boys' growth was stunted from the labor.

Gingambob: seventeenth- and eighteenth-century vernacular for scrotum.

August and the Law: *Sandy*: Sandy was an enslaved New Yorker living in his master's cellar/kitchen.

Snagging Shadows: The voices are enslaved New Yorkers living in a cellar.

THE BODY'S METROPOLIS

The Body Is a Metropolis (1741 New York slave conspiracy): There were nearly a dozen fires between March 18th and April 6th of 1741. White colonists believed these fires were set by Negroes and specifically instigated by a free-spirited enslaved man named Caesar who headed a group called the "Geneva Club Negroes" who were known for filching property. Caesar's master was a baker, and Caesar had a child with an Irish woman named Peggy living with the Hughsons who owned a Broadway tippling house which some enslaved Negroes frequented. Enslaved Negroes drinking and socializing was illegal, especially after dark. As petty thieves, Caesar and his main accomplice—the enslaved Prince—worked with John Hughson, who fenced their stolen goods—during this particular heist, candlesticks, silver, and linen. Likely because of the memory of the 1712 revolt, white colonists grew hysterical after the first few 1741 blazes. A number of Negroes, free and enslaved, were rounded up, tried, and executed. Caesar and Hughson—the purported ring leaders—were both hanged, cut down, and then hung on the Collect Pond which was in the area of the Negro Burial Ground. Their bodies, left dangling for three months, putrefied.

At one point every black male sixteen and older was jailed. Over that spring and summer, thirty black men were executed at the Commons: thirteen burned at the stake and seventeen hanged. Two white women and two white men—Sarah and John Hughson were two of the four—were also executed. Peggy—Caesar's lover—was the other white woman executed.

Deal board is made out of either fir or pine wood. See Jill Lepore's fine work *New York Burning* (New York: Vintage Books, 2003) for a nuanced look at the "1741 slave riot."

A Six-Sided Cedar Coat (The Revolutionary War, New York): Lord Dunmore had been governor of both New York and Virginia but was also a loyalist faithful to the British crown. He decreed that any Negroes who fought on behalf of the English would be freed once the war ended. Enslaved and free Negroes joined the British, coming from as far away as South Carolina. Some enslaved individuals fought for both the patriots and the loyalists. Pompey Lamb, Bristol Budd, Inchu Moore, and Salem Poor were four Negroes known to have fought in New York City. Poor also fought in Massachusetts, Charlestown, and Valley Forge.

Guerrilla rangers were enslaved and free blacks fighting on behalf of the British. Some Negroes left fighting for the colonists to side with the British. The 1783 Treaty of Paris set terms which supposedly guaranteed the return of black men and women—considered "stolen property"—to the colonists, but in New York, these Negroes were under British protection. Enraged, George Washington demanded the return of "Negroes and other Property" in accordance with Article 7 of the Treaty of Paris; nevertheless, in the fall of 1783, approximately 3,000 Negroes left with the British on ships headed to various destinations in the Caribbean and Canada. George Washington owned a plantation worked by 317 enslaved individuals, 123 of which he owned.

Black Pioneers: Black soldiers/paramilitary served as guards, pilots, spies, and interpreters in all-black British companies. On the actual evacuation day, November 25, 1783, the Black Pioneers leaving with the British greased the flagpole on New York's Battery—modern-day Battery Park—to slow the removal of the Union Jack.

Tea (water): superior water pumped from New York area springs. Tea was expensive, so only the finest water was used to brew it.

"The Book of Negroes" was a list containing names of loyalists who had joined British forces during the New York campaign and whom the British commander, Sir Guy Carleton, had agreed to free. The Negro Burial Ground was divided into four quadrants, largely by the periods when the largest numbers of burials seemingly occurred. The cemetery's last quadrant—the Kalk Hook (Dutch for "chalk" or "shell" hill) Farm—was located in the northwest, and those final burials (1776–1795) had an unusually large number of grown men buried without coffins (twenty-one out of the thirty-two coffinless burials in the entire cemetery). Archaeologists and anthropologists deduced that these men had fought for the British during the Revolutionary War and were stricken with smallpox. The outbreak, shortage of wood, and absence of local family likely led to burial without coffins. Most of these men had come to New York when Lord Dunmore put out the call for Negroes willing to aid the British during their seven-year occupation. A New York Historical Society document mentions "an aged gentleman who remembers Negroes from Virginia were encamped in this area on an open field. They got smallpox, died in great numbers and were buried in the negro ground."

British copper coins were often placed on the eyes of the deceased as a burial tribute that also kept the deceased's eyelids closed. Burial #6 was an approximately forty-year-old Negro who was six feet tall and likely a Revolutionary War soldier. On his torso were gold and pewter buttons (one with an anchor and rope insignia worn by British sailors during the Revolution), a long coat, winding sheet, and British sailor's outfit.

Frog Hall was loyalist and New York Supreme Court Chief Justice Daniel Horsmanden's house, seized by General George Washington and converted into a hospital.

Washington had thought to burn the city down before the British captured it in September 1776. On September 21, fires raged across Manhattan. Five hundred buildings—more than a quarter of the city—burned down. Two hundred patriots were arrested and American spy Nathan Hale was hanged.

The epigraph is a poem from the *New York Journal* newspaper (May 25, 1776) that took a swipe at Lord Dunmore's policy of enlisting Negroes to assist the British.

Feet-Me-Downs: Until after the Civil War, shoes were not made as lefts and rights but rather with straight soles. Nigger Brogans were slaves' shoes. They might be placed on the feet for a funeral ceremony but were afterward removed and given to individuals whose feet were the same size.

Juba is a type of dance with African roots that enslaved folks performed, accompanied by complex rhythmic hand clapping and slapping of the knees and thighs.

Boneyard: graveyard

Kith: When Caesar and John Hughson were chained and hung on gibbets for eleven weeks on the isle in the Collect Pond, Caesar allegedly began to "look white," while Hughson began to "look black," his hair coiling, nose flattening, and lips thickening.

Monmouth cap: men's knitted, round, woolen headgear—fashionable between the fifteenth and eighteenth centuries.

BONEYARNS

In this section, I imagined "talking to these bones" and questioning these eighteenth century "ancestors." Responses reflect both the bones and their souls answering.

Spirit of an enslaved New York woman shot and killed, Burial #25: Forensic specialists determined she was an adult female who had died from a musket ball still lodged in her rib cage centuries later. They also found her buried "above" an enslaved man's casket.

Columbia University Graverobbers #2: The graverobbing took place at night and the bodies were used for anatomy class.

To the Bones: About the Beads: Talking: Beads were found on and around the bones of some of the enslaveds' skeletons. The beads referred to were located in Burial #107, the grave of a forty-year-old woman.

To the Bones: About the Beads: Talking: (beads as funerary objects in Burial #340). Nankeen breeches were durable, brownish-yellow cotton pants originally made in China.

To the Bones: About the Beads: Talking (Burial #340): Important symbols worn in West Africa for centuries, beads were used to keep wearers from harm and help them make the journey into the afterlife.

Burial #340 was interred with 111 waist beads, which in certain African societies indicated the importance of the wearer. She might have been the daughter of a king or chief or knowledgeable about remedies and healing. Her Linsey apron, however, was a badge of slavery. The enslaved received clothes as allotments and cut and sewed their own clothes. Linsey was inexpensive, durable, coarse linen.

Talking to the Bones: Only nine of the 146 beads found in the Negro Burial Ground were made in Africa—Ghana, specifically. Eight were located in Burial #226 around the neck of a child under two months old. Her coffin was situated inside a 30–60-year-old man's grave, Burial #221.

Talking to the Teeth: (Burial #340): Some of the dead's teeth were sculpted into various shapes, indicating the deceased were likely born in Africa. Analysis of teeth and bones of many of the children's burials indicated poor nutrition and a limited diet high in sugar, corn, and flour.

Talking to the Bones: Talking (souls of enslaved two-year-olds): There were infants buried amongst the dead, some as young as two months old.

Talking to the Bones: Talking: Bones were sometimes discovered in odd places on a skeleton. In the case of this grave, a forearm was placed where a shin should be. What the forensic specialists were unable to determine is whether this placement happened as a result of urban development or something that might have been the cause of death. There were also indications of extraordinary stresses on bones from heavy and consistent lifting—even children. The Akan-speaking Coromantee were from what is now Ghana. At times, forensic specialists were able to determine that the enslaved who lived to adulthood frequently grew up in Africa, whereas the children's skeletons often belonged to individuals who had been born here. They attribute the high incidence of childhood deaths to poor diet and overwork.

Talking to the Bones: Talking (spirit of a skull facing west): In many west African societies, the tradition was to bury an individual with the head facing west, in the direction of the setting sun.

JUPITER & WHEATLEY'S SUITE

Jupiter Hammon (living in Queens Village, New York): In 1760, Jupiter Hammon was the first Negro to publish poetry in the United States, in a broadside entitled: "An Evening Prayer Salvation by Christ with Penitential Cries: Composed by Jupiter Hammon, a Negro belonging to Mr. Lloyd of Queen's Village." In the South, it was illegal for a Negro to read or write and punishments were severe; Hammon's writings were therefore revolutionary. Born in New York in 1711, he would have been considered a house servant and for an enslaved individual lived a charmed life, taught to read and write by the Lloyd family. Growing up, he also played with the children in their Horse Neck Manor house. The Lloyds recognized his intelligence and let him transact business such as collecting quitrent from tenant farmers. He also engaged in his own small businesses, selling fruit, needles, and Bibles. He pocketed his earnings or was paid by the family. Jupiter worked for four generations of Lloyds. His father, Obadiah, had been abducted in Africa, brought to the colonies in a slave ship, and sold to the family, who also taught him to read and write.

Homespun is loosely woven wool or linen made from yarn.

Tinged: During the Revolutionary War, Jupiter Hammon fled with the Lloyds to Connecticut, where in 1778 he wrote a poem entitled "An Address to Miss Phillis Wheatley." Hammon questioned Wheatley's Christian faith yet never the faith of his white owners.

Guineaman was another name for a slave ship.

Below are lines adapted from Hammon's poem:

For this cottage
of clay . . . touched by . . . redeeming . . . grace
conned from . . . heathen shores . . . by
the Lord's shepherd.

An Almost Audience: Phillis Wheatley was likely abducted from modern-day Senegal. Initially brought to the Caribbean on a slave ship called the "Phillis," she was eventually taken to New England, as were some enslaved individuals deemed too infirm for work in the South. Captain Peter Gwinn commanded the ship, owned by merchant Timothy Fitch, that brought her to Massachusetts. Phillis was sold to Boston merchant and tailor John Wheatley. Pre-pubescent girls like her were the least valued as they could not work like boys, women, or men, nor were they yet of child-bearing age. Unable to get her book published in the colonies, she traveled at the age of twenty, accompanied by the Wheatleys' son Nathaniel, to London where she had audiences with the Lord Mayor and Selina Hastings, Countess of Huntingdon, who facilitated the publication in 1773 of *Poems on Various Subjects, Religious and Moral*. Phillis dedicated the collection to her. In 1775, Phillis sent a copy of a poem titled "To His Excellency, George Washington" to the general, and in March of the next year, he invited her to his headquarters in Cambridge, Massachusetts. She was freed upon her master's death.

Worthies: white men of means and social standing. Many white colonists did not believe Phillis actually wrote her poems but parroted somebody else's words. She, however, was writing poems in iambic pentameter by age fourteen. Two of Wheatley's children died at a young age. Her free but poor husband, John Peters, was imprisoned for debt in 1784, leaving an impoverished Wheatley with a sickly infant son; thereafter, she went to work as a scullery maid at a boarding house.

Boston's Old South Meeting House was a church Phillis attended on Washington and Milk Streets.

Sable Marginalia: If an enslaved or free Negro published a book, he or she needed attestation from whites that the words published were actually those of the Negro. Wheatley's poems were vetted by Boston luminaries John Erving,

Reverend Charles Chauncey, John Hancock, Governor Thomas Hutchinson of Massachusetts, and his lieutenant governor, Andrew Oliver.

FREEDOM SUITE

Coating: *Warwick*: (a formerly enslaved Negro, New York, eighteenth century): Freed Negroes still suffered under restrictive laws such as curfews.

Bill of Sale: Freed Negroes often had to carry "bills of sale" indicating they or someone had purchased their freedom so they would not be either re-enslaved or imprisoned. Both enslaved and free Negroes outside after dark had to carry lanterns so they could be identified by colonists.

Long in That Late-Afternoon Light: *Bukay* (free New York sailor, 1780): One of the interesting occupations of enslaved and free Negro males was working as sailors; although the enslaved could have escaped while in Europe, they often returned to the Americas.

Charade clubs: costume parties
Airs. Fin'ries: dressy or showy clothing and jewels
Baize: a coarse woolen or cotton fabric napped to imitate felt
Mantua: a loose-fitting gown

Full Out: *Richard* (free New York Negro, 1810s): Names given to slaves by masters were frequently nicknames or mispronunciations of the enslaved's African name, such as "Quock" for the Akan name "Kwaku." Freed slaves often chose new names as symbols of freedom and autonomy.

Wool: vernacular description of the texture of Richard's hair. Enslaved Negroes sometimes braided their hair and secured it with dried eel.

Kin: *Quack* (enslaved New Yorker, eighteenth century): "Word House" was a neologism or slang for "dictionary."

STOCKS AND BONDAGE: WALL STREET

(two centuries/three parts)

A. Construction: In 1653, enslaved Negroes built a defensive wall that extended river to river with logs twelve feet long and eighteen inches in circumference that kept Native Americans and the English out of the Dutch colony of New Amsterdam. Between the former barricades, *Walstraat* may have been named for an earthen embankment at the northern boundary or for the Walloons, thirty settler families that embarked on the *Nieu Nederlandt* in 1624. Peter Minuit, the colonist who "bought" Manhattan from Native Americans, was Walloon. On English maps, the street appeared as "de Walstraat" or "Waal Straat." Manhattan Island's "red people" crossed to the mainland and made a treaty with the Dutch in a place called the Pipe of Peace—Hoboken in the native language. The Dutch Director-General, William Kieft, then sent colonists to massacre the native population. The Dutch used slave labor to erect a double palisade, which became the northern boundary of the city, for defense against retaliation.

B. Auction: Hell's Unbidden Hello (New York City slave market, 1711–1762): Even before they could see the vessels, workers could smell the odor from unsanitary conditions in the holds. Ships docked at Water Street Pier 17, called the Old Slip. Before the auction, newly-arrived Africans' bodies were inspected by prospective buyers. Colonists believed that salty sweat meant illness.

C. Buttonwood Agreement (May 1792): Twenty-four colonists (stockbrokers and merchants) met under a buttonwood (sycamore) tree to sign "The Buttonwood Agreement" and become the first members of the New York Stock Exchange; thereafter, these men traded financial instruments on commodities such as cotton, ships, insurance, and slaves. The tree was located just outside 68 Wall Street where the current New York Stock Exchange sits. Not a block away stood the slave market.

VIII

An Honorable Harvest: In 1785, the New York Manumission Society was created to emancipate enslaved New Yorkers and promote their welfare. More than half the members, including John Jay, John Lamb, James Duane, and possibly Alexander Hamilton, owned slaves and yet decried slavery in the South and the Caribbean.

Ashley and New Amsterdam: Until the 1830s, New York was second only to Charleston, South Carolina (America's largest slave port), in per capita percentage of enslaved individuals.

After/thought/After/life: British colonial businesses encroached on the Negro Burial Ground which became a dumping site for tanneries, potteries, and residences. The Collect Pond (*Kalchook*, or *Kolch*, "small body of water") was the city's primary water source and bordered the cemetery. The burial ground had four sections: the Kalk Hook Form (northwest), Van Borsum Patent (private property in the southwest), the Corporation (southwest), and Janeway Land (east).

Breath's Breath: *Japhet* (enslaved New York sailor, 1774): Enslaved Negro men worked as sailors and acquired knowledge of languages in addition to several spoken in colonial New York. One, named Japhet, visited Cadiz and La Caleta, Spain, where the Tavira tower was located. Mulberry and Orange were street names in Manhattan.

A Clockwise Tizzy (slave funeral): Bodies of enslaved were often wrapped in linen secured with brass pins. Coffins were frequently hexagonal or four-sided and tapered. Conjure bundles were believed to possess spiritual power. A broken stoneware vessel placed on the coffin lid of Burial #328 (a woman between 40 and 50 years) contained a blue spiral on the bottom, a motif depicting a Kongo cosmogram, symbol of cyclical connection between the realms of the living and the dead. Markings were thought to indicate where a Kongo spirit may land upon the physical world. Four phases represented are birth, life, death, and rebirth. Blue symbolized water, delineating the land of their ancestors and connoting passage to the realm of the dead or the world of the spirits. Following the 1712 revolt, colonists instituted more slave codes, such as allowing only twelve Negroes to attend a funeral and prohibiting night burials that were the custom of many West African cultures, because they feared that night gatherings might lead to plots of slave revolts. During funerals, mourners circumnavigated the coffin in a clockwise direction, drummed, wailed, and passed a newborn over the lid.

First and Final: Joshua Delaplaine was a Quaker cabinetmaker (1720–1778). Some masters paid him to build coffins for their enslaved dead, almost never giving names but only general descriptions such as "coffin for his negro boy." Of the thirteen slave coffins he constructed, he was given only three first names of Negro women—Molly, rozind, and Jane. The only first and last names of an enslaved individual Delaplaine recorded in his account book is "Joseph Castins," whose owner, Caleb Lawrence, requested a "9 shilling, rough coffin" for this man in July 1755. No other grave markers have names, so Joseph Castins held a unique place among the 15,000 interred.

This Is Sorcery (April 6, 1712, New York slave revolt): A group of twenty-four enslaved Negroes, Spanish Indians, and some Native Americans plotted to set fire to colonial baker Peter Van Tilburg's outhouse, hoping to draw colonists outside where the conspirators planned to murder them using muskets, hatchets, swords, and knives. They hoped that many other enslaved people would join their revolt. They succeeded in killing nine colonists and wounding six. After the revolt was quelled, some conspirators tried to escape to the woods beyond Maiden Lane, but seventeen were captured by Governor Robert Hunter's soldiers while six committed suicide. Seventy Negroes were arrested in all: forty-three were tried and twenty-five convicted. Twenty were hanged, three were burned alive at the stake, one was broken on the wheel, and one roasted to death. Some convicted were later found to be innocent. Governor Hunter, appalled by the executions, released the last five conspirators, including a Spanish Native American named Josey and a

Spanish Negro named Juan who were free men who had been sold into slavery. Kip was a street in lower Manhattan. Cuffee, Quito, Mingo, Quack, and Quash were common African names.

I. *Incantation*: The only free Negro conspirator in the 1712 revolt, Peter the Doctor, was an African *Nganga* (spiritual diviner) who gave the participants a *minkisi* (conjure bundle believed to be imbued with powers from the ancestral world) which, when rubbed on their bodies, would make them invisible and shield them from bullets. Interestingly, none of them was shot or killed during the uprising. He was acquitted and discharged. Cuffee, from Ghana, and Spanish Juan, who had been taken from a privateer in 1706, set ablaze the house of their master, Peter Van Tilburg. Spanish Negroes were free seamen taken from ships captured by the British in the eighteenth century and enslaved although they protested that they were free citizens. Peter the Porter, owned by Andries Maerschalck, killed young Joris (Andries' son), a brutal slave owner, with a dagger.

Spatterdash: garments made from wool, linen, or leather worn by sporting gentlemen, laborers, or military men which covered the leg from mid-shin to the top of the foot.

II. *Invitation*: Tom, owned by Nicholas Roosevelt, shot Andries Beekman in the chest and was tried and roasted in slow torment. Amba, owned by Adolphus Phillipse, was tried, acquitted, and discharged. Of three women involved, Lilly, owned by John Crooke, was also acquitted.

III. *Benediction*: The 1712 revolt was the first organized slave revolt in New York. Some masters testified against their own slaves in court.

Which/One: Sarah and Abigail were enslaved women who may have participated in the 1712 revolt. Abigail was owned by Gysbert Vaninburgh, Sarah by Stophell Pels. Both were convicted and hanged. One was pregnant and allowed to live until the child's birth and then hanged in chains.

Six-week teeth: Teeth begin to develop in a fetus after six weeks.

"Playing the Lady": Enslaved women sometimes emphasized their pregnancies and suckling in order to get reduced workloads and more food.

The quickening, the first noticeable movement of a fetus, begins in the second trimester.

Knowery is enslaved vernacular for knowledge, often centered around birthing.

Black haw is a hawthorn berry used for preventing miscarriage and uterine spasms following childbirth.

Blue cohosh is a Native American plant used to induce/augment labor and reduce birth pains.

A lying-in room was postpartum bedrest/confinement which slaveowners allowed some enslaved women.

Which, Too/Split Flash: New York's earliest prison was situated in the cellar of City Hall, also the location of the mayoral residence, Supreme Court, whipping posts, and pillories on the corner of Broad and Wall Streets in 1699. Constructed of stone that enslaved Africans had used to build the seventeenth-century Dutch barricade, City Hall is located on the same site. Prisoners were bound in iron shackles stapled to the walls of the dungeon. Pregnant women often lie on their left sides to alleviate pain during the third trimester.

Bench wig: white perukes worn by judges in the colonies and England

Necessary (ordure) tub: a large bucket in which human excrement was evacuated

III Sundered: In many West African countries, children were named for the day of the week on which they were born. The enslaved sometimes ate dirt to supplement their diets, induce abortion, or suspend ovulation. Enslaved children could be put to work as early as the age of three.

Veil over the Face: African folk belief that a child born with the placenta over its face will be able to "see the future."

Beriberi, a deficiency disease caused by undernourishment in the womb, causes inflammation of nerves, digestive system, and heart and can lead to blindness. Many slave children were born underweight because of their mothers' poor nutrition.

Talking to the Bones (spirit of an enslaved New York woman with a pipe beside her skeleton, Burial #340): The Norfleet cotton plantation was located in Tarboro, North Carolina. Burial with personal effects was an African custom. One name for a pipe was *Ebua*.

Day's end.: Because the enslaved toiled all day and rarely had weekends off, night might be the only time a proper burial could take place. Masters and city fathers rarely attended.